At school

Bobbie Kalman

🌳 Crabtree Publishing Company

www.crabtreebooks.com

Created by Bobbie Kalman

**Author and
Editor-in-Chief**
Bobbie Kalman

Reading consultant
Elaine Hurst

Editors
Kathy Middleton
Crystal Sikkens
Joan King

Special thanks to
Jennifer King, Educational consultant

Design
Bobbie Kalman
Katherine Berti

**Production coordinator
and Prepress technician**
Katherine Berti

Photo research
Bobbie Kalman

Photographs
Digital Stock: page 6
Other photographs by Shutterstock

Library and Archives Canada Cataloguing in Publication

Kalman, Bobbie, 1947-
    At school / Bobbie Kalman.

(My world)
ISBN 978-0-7787-9497-4 (bound).--ISBN 978-0-7787-9522-3 (pbk.)

    1. Schools--Juvenile literature. 2. School day--Juvenile literature.
I. Title. II. Series: My world (St. Catharines, Ont.)

LB1513.K33 2011   j372   C2010-901967-9

Library of Congress Cataloging-in-Publication Data

Kalman, Bobbie.
 At school / Bobbie Kalman.
    p. cm. -- (My world)
 ISBN 978-0-7787-9522-3 (pbk. : alk. paper) -- ISBN 978-0-7787-9497-4
(reinforced library binding : alk. paper)
 1. Schools--Juvenile literature. 2. School day--Juvenile literature. I. Title.
II. Series.

 LB1513.K33 2010
 372--dc22

                                                            2010011297

Crabtree Publishing Company

Printed in China/072010/AP20100226

www.crabtreebooks.com   1-800-387-7650

**Published in Canada
Crabtree Publishing**
616 Welland Ave.
St. Catharines, Ontario
L2M 5V6

**Published in the United States
Crabtree Publishing**
PMB 59051
350 Fifth Avenue, 59th Floor
New York, New York 10118

**Published in the United Kingdom
Crabtree Publishing**
Maritime House
Basin Road North, Hove
BN41 1WR

**Published in Australia
Crabtree Publishing**
386 Mt. Alexander Rd.
Ascot Vale (Melbourne)
VIC 3032

Words to know

count

draw

eat

have fun

learn

listen

make music

paint

play

read

talk

write

I read at school.

I write at school.

I play at school.

I count at school.

I draw at school.

I paint at school.

I listen at school.

I talk at school.

I eat at school.

I make music at school.

I learn at school.

I have fun with my friends at school.

Notes for adults

Objectives
- to help children learn the important verbs related to school: read, write, play, count, draw, paint, listen, talk, make music, learn, eat, and have fun
- to create an imaginative community for learning through spoken, written, and visual activities

Before reading the book
Write these frequently used words on the board: I, at, school

Ask the children these questions:
"Why are you at school?" (to learn)
"What are two important things you will learn at school?" (read and write)
"How do you find out how many of an object there is?" (count)
"Which two things do you do in art?" (draw and paint)
"What do you do at recess?" (play, have fun)
"What do you do at lunchtime?" (eat)
"What do you do when the teacher is speaking?" (listen)
"What do you do when you answer a question?" (talk)
"How do you make music at school?" (sing, play musical instruments)

After reading the book
Ask the children:
"What kinds of things do you learn at school?"
"What kinds of things do you learn at home?"
"Where else do you learn?" (daycare, grandparents' home, church/temple/mosque, etc.)
"What do you want to learn that you have not learned yet?"

Activity
Ask each child to paint or draw a picture of a favorite thing that s/he is learning at school. Print one sentence under the illustration, using the name of the student who drew the picture. i.e. "Jennifer counts at school."
"Jamie writes at school."

Assemble all the children's pages into a book. Place the book in the library for other children to enjoy.

Extension
Read *My school community* to the children and ask them how the people in their school community help them learn.

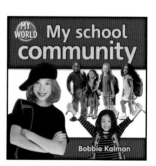

Guided Reading: G

For teacher's guide, go to www.crabtreebooks.com/teachersguides